Super Bears

MIKE SINGLETARY

By Paul J. Deegan

Abdo & Daughters
Minneapolis

Published by Abdo & Daughters, 6537 Cecilia Circle, Minneapolis, Minnesota 55435

Library bound edition distributed by Rockbottom Books, Pentagon Tower, P.O. Box 36036, Minneapolis, Minnesota 55435

Paperback edition distributed by Contemporary Books, Inc., 180 North Michigan Avenue, Chicago, Illinois 60601.

Copyright © 1986 by Abdo Consulting Group, Inc., Minneapolis, Minnesota. International copyrights reserved in all countries. No part of this book may be reproduced in any form without written permission from the publisher. Printed in the United States.

Library of Congress Number: 86-71849   ISBN: 0-939179-06-7
                                                (Library Bound)

                                           0-939179-13-X
                                             (Paperback)

Photos — cover and inside pages: Jonathan Daniel
back cover: John Biever

The Chicago Bears dream season of 1985 began on a college campus in Platteville, Wisconsin. The team had gathered there for summer training camp. There they chanted, "From Second Street to Bourbon Street."

Second Street was the football camp at the University of Wisconsin-Platteville. Bourbon Street is in New Orleans, the site of Super Bowl XX to be played six months later.

When Super Bowl Sunday came, the Bears were there. In no small part thanks to a hardnosed middle linebacker. Mike Singletary is a man who relishes putting his helmet on the numbers. He is a standout in what many believe is pro football's best defense ever.

Mike Singletary is "the man who puts all the parts together" for the Chicago Bears defense. That's what Bears head coach Mike Ditka says.

Could this be the same Mike Singletary people knew as a boy in Houston, Texas?

Surely it was, although no one who knew him as a young boy could possibly have imagined that he would someday be the National Football League

(NFL) Defensive Player of the Year in both 1984 and 1985.

You see, young Mike Singletary was considered too unhealthy, too frail, to take part in sports.

Also, his father, Charles, was a Pentecostal minister. For many years he refused to let Mike or his nine older brothers and sisters take part in sports or dress and undress for gym classes.

Today, Singletary says that his father "was very strict." He has said his father related everything to his understanding of religious principles. The family sometimes spend 12 hours in church on Sunday according to Singletary.

If his father's attitude had been different, Mike wouldn't have had an early start in athletics anyway. He has recalled having pneumonia three or four times along with other illnesses. "I remember going to the hospital every other day until I was seven or eight years old," he told a reporter.

However, even as a young boy, Singletary loved football. It has been written that at age 12 he wanted to run away from home so he could play football.

Even in junior high school, today's Bears defensive captain was only 5-4 and 120 pounds. The local school coaches were not camping on his doorstep.

Then two things happened.

His father changed his mind about sports. And Mike grew some five inches in one year and began adding pounds. He began playing football. He was a linebacker from day one.

He has recalled that only one thing was tough. "The other kids understood more than I did. I didn't know everybody had a position he was responsible for."

He made up for this by hard work. This is a habit he has carried with him throughout his football career. He has said he attributes his work habits "to my upbringing."

"My mother and father spent a lot of time with me because I was the last of 10 kids, I guess. They rushed through the first nine and then took time with me and did it right.

"My mother would sit down with me sometimes, times when I could have been playing around the corner. She'd tell me what life was all about. How easily things can be taken away from you. How you can't take anything for granted.

"She taught me to keep working."

The fact that he was smaller than most kids motivated Mike. "Every year I wanted to get out and prove something else," he has said. "I can do this. I will do this."

"I'd look at a guy who was six-feet-three and 240 pounds and I'd say, 'I can do that better.' It's not size. It's desire. I think my lack of size gave me the drive to prove it, show it, do it."

Mike went on to play at Houston's Worthing High School. During high school he turned the garage at home into a summer weight-training facility. He opened it to other kids. The school's basketball coach even sent his players there!

Singletary went to college at Baylor University. He became a starter midway through his freshman year. He finished his college career as a consensus All-American. Singletary was the Southwest Conference's Player of the Year as a junior and senior. Such an award usually goes to an offensive player.

Three times while playing for the Waco, Texas, school, Singletary had 30 or more tackles in a game. He averaged 15 per game for his career. When he was a freshman in 1978, Baylor changed their defense to take better advantage of Singletary's play.

Singletary had made his mark in the always strong Southwest Conference. Still, he did go until the second round of the 1981 NFL draft. The prototype National Football League middle linebacker should be six-feet-two or six-feet-three. Singletary is a shade under six-feet. The Bears believed he should have been drafted late in the first round. They were happy he was still available in the second round.

However, as a new Bear, Singletary's relationship with the Bears defensive coordinator Buddy Ryan was not always pleasant. Ryan is a coach of the past in that he doesn't worry about wounding a player's feelings.

The story is told of an incident during Singletary's rookie season in 1981. Ryan removed Mike from a game. He watched from the sidelines, then approached Ryan. He told the coach he knew what he had done wrong, and asked if he should go back in the game. Ryan is said to have told him, "No, no, son. We're going to try to win this game."

Singletary did not become a starter until midway through his rookie year. Even then, it is said, Ryan did not let Singletary play on third downs or in other obvious passing situations for almost two years.

Singletary said during the 1985 season that he "didn't like Buddy very much at first. But there's nothing I wouldn't do for him now.

"When he comes up to you and says, 'I guess I had you wrong. I really thought you could do the job,' you like to die. I'm not playing for my family or Chicago," Singletary told a magazine writer, "but for him (Ryan)."

When it became apparent during the days before the 1986 Super Bowl that Ryan probably would be leaving to accept a head coaching job, Singletary said he couldn't sleep the night before the game thinking about Ryan leaving.

The feeling is mutual. Ryan once said, "Every coach ought to get a chance to coach a guy like that."

Singletary caused Ryan to change his mind because the coach saw the young player's dedication. Following his rookie season with the Bears, Singletary returned to Waco. There he spent hours

watching films. More hours were spent on the Baylor practice field where he worked on his pass drops.

It took until 1983, however, before Singletary was in the game on every defensive play.

Two more years and the Bears defense was awesome on occasion. Take November 17, 1985 in Texas Stadium in Dallas. The Bears shut out the Cowboys 44-0. It was the worst defeat ever for Dallas. The Bears regular quarterback Jim McMahon didn't even dress for the game. He had an injured right shoulder.

The defense scored 14 of the Chicago points. Twice during the game, the Bears defense knocked Dallas quarterback Danny White out of the game. He and backup Gary Hogeboom could complete only six passes in 22 attempts. They were sacked six times.

The Bears had lost six straight to Dallas before this game. On this Sunday they stunted their linemen and raised havoc in the Cowboys backfield. They blitzed linebackers, safeties, and Singletary. The defense had one objective: Get to the quarterback.

Many coaches want their pass rushers to stay in lanes. The Bears simply went after their quarry — White or Hogeboom.

Following the game, Dallas coaches said the shifting by the Bears defense caused them a lot of problems. Singletary told writers that the key to the defense's success that day was "our guys get off the ball so fast."

He said the Bears defense is constant movement. "They call an audible, we move. It's tough to make an adjustment when someone is moving."

Singletary told a reporter, "A lot of people were saying, 'Now the defense has to go out and score points because McMahon's out.' But that wasn't it.

"It was just a matter of playing the kind of defense we're capable of playing. We're still getting better." Singletary said the defense wanted to reach its peak "at the right time, and that's going into the playoffs."

After he had become a starter, Singletary had a goal of making it to the Pro Bowl. He did that in 1983 and was a starter for the National Conference team the following three years.

Then his goal was to be named the consensus NFL Defensive Player of the Year. This he accomplished in 1985. He did it by often showing up at the Bears training facility on Tuesday. That's a day off for the players. He would come to pick up the game plan from Ryan. This meant he would know what was going to happen in Wednesday's practice.

"The way I look at it, you have to do that kind of thing if you're going to succeed," Singletary said. "If you come in on Wednesday and start studying the game plan, Tuesday is gone. Tuesday is the day to get rid of soreness and to get an idea of the game plan we're going to use."

The teenager who didn't know much about football today is an expert. He has to know a lot and make several instant decisions on each play.

The Bears basic defense under former defensive coordinator Buddy Ryan was called the "46" defense. The number meant nothing except that it was the uniform number worn by onetime Bears safety Doug Plank. The "46" is a complicated defense.

The basic formation in this defense calls for Singletary to line up over the opponent's right tackle. He is a few yards off the line of scrimmage. All four of the Bears down linemen are to his right. An outside linebacker is to his left.

Depending on the offensive formation and play choice, Singletary can be called upon to do one of several things when the ball is snapped.

He may drop back, short or deep, in pass coverage on a wide receiver.

He may cover the wide receiver if he runs a pass route just over the middle.

He may cover the tight end running a route down field.

He may have to quickly retreat to take over the free safety position.

He may blitz to the inside of the opposing tackle. He may blitz to the outside of the tackle.

What he does and where he goes is a decision he must make almost instantly.

Singletary calls the defensive signals for the Bears. Some have said he can predict what play an opponent will run. He has said that "It's not so much predicting plays as when they get in a certain formation you know what they're going to do."

Singletary said that Ryan made the defensive players' jobs easy. "He tells us what they're going to do and 99.9 percent of the time he's right."

Others give Singletary more credit for the Bears success in shutting down opposing offenses. New England Patriots defensive coordinator Red Rust says that to make the "46" defense succeed, "they need a middle linebacker who can do what Singletary does."

Singletary is able to play as many roles on defense as he does because he has exceptional speed for a big man. Probably no other linebacker even would try to go deep with a wide receiver.

Singeltary loves his position. Linebacker, he has said, is "Where you have all the controls. Where you feel the power."

He also has great confidence in his abilities. "Out on the field," Ryan once told a reporter, "you can hear him yelling, 'Come to me! Come to me!'" Ryan says he's heard other players say they want the action to come to them. However, the coach said, Singletary "is the only one who means it."

Minnesota Vikings head coach Jerry Burns coached with Ryan when Ryan was on the Vikings staff before moving to the Bears. Burns says the Bears defense works because "they have excellent people."

Burns says the best of these is Singletary.

Noting that he's been coaching for more than 30 years, Burns says "Singletary is the best tackler I've seen. There have been a lot of good ones. This guy's the best. He doesn't miss. He's deadly."

The Bears call Singletary "Samurai." A Samurai was a professional warrior in a Japanese society of long ago. His teammates hung the name on him because he made so many noises during practice.

Today Singletary is a professional football warrior. He is not huge as football players go. Remember, he was considered short for a linebacker. Not quite six feet, he plays at a compact 225 pounds.

On the field he plays with tremendous intensity — some would say like a wild man. He begins building for the game in the locker room. It is said he has gotten so worked up he has thrown a chair across the room.

That abandon goes onto the field with him. While playing at Baylor, he made enough hard hits to break 16 helmets. Now the entire Baylor team only produces two or three broken helmets a year. It was written that he rotated helmets in practice. Thus, he would have a new helmet ready to use when he broke one during a game.

The story is told of a game at Baylor when he tackled a Georgia ball carrier after smashing down two linemen leading the runner. This he did bareheaded. His helmet had come off during the play.

Singletary's tackling technique is not what one would recommend to young players. "I try to visualize my head all the way through the man," Singletary told a national magazine writer. He said he visualizes "my whole body through him."

Singletary said his high school coach told him he preferred he hit with his shoulder. "But if you want to hit with your head, do it right," the coach told him.

People in sports medicine would skip the second part of the coach's advice. The tackler who hits with his head can break his neck.

Singletary, who has a 20-inch neck, told the writer that "It's technique." It's not safe or legal unless you do it right. In fact, it's very dangerous.

"The worst thing you can do," he said, "is to lower your head when you're making a tackle. The neck, I don't care how strong, can be injured. You must keep you face back, your head up."

"Whenever I'm working (playing football)," Singletary recently told a reporter, "I'm very intense. I'm like a wild man because I want to be the best."

Fortunately for the Bears, helmets worn by NFL players are apparently more durable than those Singletary wore at Baylor.

Despite his ferocity on the field, Singletary has a reputation for being a clean player. He does not take cheap shots. He has been known to apologize to an opposing player for what he considered a sloppy tackle.

According to Ditka, Singletary "is a leader by example. The coach cited Singletary's "intensity, his zeal to do everything perfectly."

Ditka called his star linebacker "the leader of our football team. He's a solid football player who turned in another great year. He's a student of the game, a great example to his teammates and to the fans. He is very coachable."

Away from the field, Singletary does not look like a tough guy. There is a studious appearance behind the rose-tinted glasses he wears. He enjoys soft music, long walks, and reading books.

"I guess I have a split personality," he once said of the two contrasting images.

His wife, Kim, says it took her awhile to understand the two contrasting personalities. Kim, who was also a Baylor student, has said she now knows how nice her husband is off the field. On the field, it isn't anger that drives Mike, she said.

"It's just the will to be the best," Kim said.

When he gets too wound up thinking about defenses for an upcoming game, he winds down by taking long walks and listening to what he terms "quiet" music. Mike and Kim have no children yet.

Thus, there were few family responsibilities to hinder Singletary's preparation for the playoffs following the 15-1 1985 regular season. He and his defensive teammates prepared well. In three games they allowed only a field goal and a meaningless score to the New England Patriots in the Super Bowl. They shut out their first two playoff opponents.

The first round 21-0 victory over the New York Giants prompted Singletary to call the game the defense's best effort so far in the season. He said he would grade the performance an 8½ on a scale of 10.

During the Bears shutout of the Los Angeles Rams in the 1985 National Football Conference title game, the second playoff game, Singletary was at his best.

The Rams had a third down and one yard to go for a first down near midfield late in the first quarter of the January 12, 1986, contest. The Rams trailed only 10-0. Their great running back Eric Dickerson bounced outside with a handoff. From his linebacker's position, Singletary moved with him.

As he said after the game, "When he bounced, I bounced. I'm looking for him. Then we met."

Dickerson weighs 220 pounds, almost as much as Singletary. But he didn't move Mike when they met. Mike wrapped him up and took him to the ground. Dickerson lost a yard on the play and the Rams had to punt.

This was "the biggest play of the day." That was the opinion of coach Ryan.

Later in the game, Singletary rammed into Rams quarterback Dieter Brock. The ball came loose. Bears linebacker Wilber Marshall took the the fumble 52 yards for the final TD in the 24-0 shutout.

Singletary rammed into a few other people that afternoon. During the game he jarred loose screws attaching the face mask to his helmet. The chin strap broke. And though he didn't know it during the game, the helmet itself was broken.

After the game, Singletary felt very good. "By the end of the game," he told reporters, "the snow was falling harder and it was great. It really kinda brought back Christmas."

Two weeks later in Super Bowl XX, Mike set a Super Bowl record by recovering two fumbles. One came late in the first quarter with the Bears up only 6-3. Singletary fell on the loose ball at the New England 13-yard line. Two carries later, Matt Suhey had a touchdown. The Bears were on their way to a 46-10 win.

"I saw the fear in his eyes," Singletary told reporters after the game for the NFL championship. He was talking about New England's Tony Eason. The Patriots quarterback was yanked from the game after being sacked three times while failing to complete any of six passes. "We got to him early and I think he got rattled," Singletary said.

"That's when I said, 'Let's go get him.' The look in his eyes said, 'I hope we're not in for another one of these (trouncings).'"

Of course they were. As Patriots head coach Raymond Berry said of the game, "We got our rear ends handed to us."

How does Singletary feel about what the Bears defense accomplished in 1985?

First of all, he has said, it is the result of a team effort. He said that coach Ditka emphasized the TEAM in the 1985 summer training camp. "We knew all along," Singletary said, "if we just played for one another, everything would work out."

And work out it did.

There will be new challenges for the players on the Bears defense. Ryan left the Bears after the 1986 Super Bowl to become head coach of the Philadelphia Eagles. There is a new defensive coordinator. Coach Ditka has said the "Bear" defense will replace the "46" alignment.

But Singletary has his own knowledge on which he can rely. He has been known to spend three to four hours a night watching an opponents' game films.

And coach Ditka is counting on Singletary to help with the necessary adjustments. "He is going to be instrumental in helping us put in the new defensive system," the Bears head coach said.

Coach Ditka has called Singletary "a good leader and a good person. He is a great football player. He sets a great example for young people on our team, including the coaches.

Following the 1986 Super Bowl victory, Singletary said that it would be unfair to say the Bears were better than past great NFL defensive teams. He cited the Dallas Cowboys "Doomsday" defense, the Pittsburgh Steelers "Steel Curtain", and the Minnesota Vikings "Purple People Eaters."

However, Singletary did say, "I think we will be seen as one of the best teams of all time."

Probably true, and if so it will be because Singletary was the captain of one of the greatest defensive teams of all time.

And he has the memory of that one day —

Ten, nine, eight, seven, six, five, four, three, two, one . . .

The seconds ticked off the game clock in the New Orleans Superdome. Super Bowl XX was history and Mike Singletary was a member of a Super Bowl championship team.

Pleasantview Media Center
District #47
Sauk Rapids, MN 56379